Tilly's Tale

Inquiries should be addressed to:

4RV Publishing LLC

PO Box 6482

Edmond, OK 73083

http://www.4rvpublishingllc.com

ISBN-13: 978-0-9818685-9-2

ISBN-10: 0-9818685-9-2

Printed in the USA

Tilly's Tale

Written by
Harry Porter

Illustrated by
Mandy Hedrick

Edmond, OK

Dedication

This book is dedicated to Tilly. She survived against the odds and is now a happy and contented dog, loved and cared for, as all dogs should be, in the bosom of a family who cares for her and appreciates her qualities as a lifelong friend. To the other dogs that make up Harry Porter's 'pack" of rescue dogs, Dylan, Penny, Alfie, Molly, Charlie, and latest additions, the puppy Snoopy, Chloe and Cassie. All have tales to tell, which will be revealed in the other books in this series. In addition, it is dedicated to rescue dogs everywhere and to those humans who take the time and have the dedication and the love to re-home and care for these forgotten friends who would otherwise meet with a fate I would hate to contemplate.

Welcome to the first of Harry Porter's Dog Tales

Tilly's Tale is the first story in the series of Harry Porter's Dog Tales, each of which tells the story of the lives of the remarkable and very individual little rescued dogs that make up this enchanting series of books. Look for the other books as they become available.

What follows, told in her own 'words,' is *Tilly's Tale*.

Chapter 1
Shivering in the Snow

Before I start this story, let me tell you who I am. My name's Tilly, and I'm four years old, about twelve inches tall, and I'm a sort of grey with a bit of white on the chest, and, oh, yes, in case I didn't mention it, I'm a dog. Not just any dog, I'm a rescue dog. What? You don't know what a rescue dog is? Well, let me tell you that a *rescued* dog is one of the luckiest dogs in the world. Why? Perhaps if I just tell you my story you'll understand what I mean, and what makes us so special, because that's what Harry, my Dad, says we rescue dogs are, *very special.*

...

I remember the thick, dark, heavy clouds hanging in the sky over the little garden. Icicles hung from the branches of the bushes planted around the borders, and the lawn had disappeared beneath its new white blanket of soft, but very cold snow. Christmas Day had passed two days before. Inside the house the owners were warm and snug, the fire in the grate keeping the cold of winter where it should be, outside.

Due to the cold, the birds failed to make an appearance to peck at the meager crumbs placed upon the bird table at the bottom of the garden. Without the sounds of their voices, an eerie silence hung over the garden, and not a living creature stirred. Well, almost.

Under the bush that had the longest branches, an evergreen with thick, heavy leaves, I lay huddled in a ball, trying to keep warm. I was freezing. My little body shivered, and I scratched at the ground with a paw, trying to make a bed of sorts in the undergrowth, in the snow and the pieces of leaf litter that lay beneath the bush. My fur was overgrown, dense and matted, a sign that I'd not been brushed or combed for a long, long time.

I peered out from beneath the bush, and frost clung to the long hairs that dangled from my chin and tail. I wondered, for perhaps the hundredth time, why I'd been cast out to live in this cold and terrible place.

Not so long ago, I lived in a warm and cozy home

with Sam. He was an old man and cuddly. I knew that he loved me. He spent most of the day with me, talking to me, giving me little biscuit treats. When he felt up to it, he'd take me for a walk in the park on a pretty red leash that he'd bought the day he took me home as a puppy. He had me a warm dog bed, one with high sides that helped keep drafts away, and gave me a soft, pink blanket I arranged with my paws into a comfortable place to sleep.

Sometimes though, old Sam would call to me at night, and I'd jump up and sleep beside him on his bed, my head resting on the pillow next to his. He gave me a cuddly toy, a little teddy bear that I proudly carried around the house with me. I would cuddle up to it at night when I wasn't lying next to Sam.

One day, Sam didn't get up. I knew something was wrong when the old man failed to give me my usual morning biscuits or to let me out in the garden to play. Sam's son and his wife came by, and I heard my name mentioned as old Sam asked his family to take care of me if anything happened to him. "His perfect little dog," he called me.

I wasn't allowed back in the house for a long time, and I didn't understand what was going on. What was wrong with Sam, my friend, my master, the one person in the world who loved me? A short time later, two men in white coats came and took Sam away on a bed with wheels, and I never saw him again.

I was left alone for almost the whole day, until Sam's son arrived at dusk. He gathered up my bed and the toys that Sam had given me. He took me and my few possessions to his house a mile away from Sam's. Instead of allowing me into the house with him, the man made me sit outside while he talked to his wife.

"I will not have that dog in the house," she shouted. "You know I can't stand animals of any kind."

"But, Dad asked me to take care of her; you know he did," the man replied.

"She stays in the garden, and that's that!" the woman said.

My tail, which I normally carried proudly curled over my back, drooped, and I let it fall between my legs. I had a feeling that things were about to change. A wave of misery washed over me as I realized that, for some reason, Sam wasn't coming back for me and that I'd arrived at a home where I wasn't wanted.

Time went by, and there I was, lying weary and sad under the bush at the bottom of the garden, day after day after day. As the cold months of winter dragged on, I always seemed to feel wet, and the cold made my body ache constantly. I cried to myself every day.

What? You didn't know dogs could cry? Well, we can, and I'd never felt so unhappy in my life. I was so alone and felt as depressed as a dog can get. Dogs feel most of the emotions that humans do, except perhaps hatred. We don't understand that one at all. How many times have dogs being shouted at or punished and then run to their human masters to try and gain affection from them? That's because our nature is essentially one of love and caring for those around us.

Perhaps the strongest emotion I felt was being unwanted. That, for a dog, is probably the worst feeling of all. Without Sam, I felt as though nobody in the whole world loved or wanted me anymore. I grieved for my old friend, and I wished for the day when someone would love me, perhaps just a little, once again.

Weeks turned to months, and I felt colder and lonelier with each passing day. My only food came from the scraps from the dinner table that Sam's son put out for me every evening. I grew thinner and thinner. There were no more biscuits, no dog treats, and no walks in the park. My lovely dog bed was long gone, sold by the woman at a market, along with my dog toys. Worst of all, I watched her throw my favorite cuddly teddy bear in to a large, black dustbin. I couldn't even cuddle up to my little bear any more.

At least, before the coldest weather of the winter came, I'd been able to sit and watch the birds each day as they landed and took off from the bird table. I enjoyed listening to their cheerful songs while they sat on the table or in the bushes or on the fence that surrounded the garden. Now that most of the birds had taken flight to warmer places for the winter, my loneliness increased. I rarely left my place under the bush. I was sad, so very sad, and didn't understand what I had done.

December passed and gave way to January. The snows came even harder and thicker, laying their soft, white, freezing blanket upon the ground. My muscles stiffened, and my body ached from the constant shivering. I barely moved any more. I tried to huddle up tight in a little ball to keep warm. I had painful sores on my tummy, probably caused by the constant dampness, and I never, ever wagged my tail.

February came, and the first signs of spring appeared. Snowdrops popped their heads through the soft earth. Birds began to come in greater numbers to the bird table. I felt that a few of my little feathered friends had returned to keep me company and to entertain me with their cheerful songs. Sometimes, on days when the sun shone and a little warmth found its way into the garden, I'd venture from under the bush and walk stiffly around the garden. I remembered the days when old Sam would take me for walks in the park, when I could feel soft, green grass beneath my paws, and when I could run and play with the other dogs I'd sometimes meet.

I did try from time to time to make friends with the woman of the house. If I saw her coming through the door, I'd walk slowly to her and look up, my tail held a little higher than usual, trying to make her aware I wanted to be friends. Instead of reaching down and stroking me, as I thought she might, or speaking softly to me as Sam would have, she'd grin at me in a cruel way and lash out with her foot, kicking me around my back legs and tail.

That really hurt, and to this day I still feel afraid when a stranger tries to touch me there. So, I'd run and hide under my bush, keeping out of sight until she'd gone. I knew that the woman hated me, but I didn't understand why. What had I done to deserve such hatred?

Sam's son would sometimes pity me and bring me a little treat, perhaps a little bone from the butcher's shop or maybe a packet of dog biscuits, giving me a few at a time. I was in a wretched state, and perhaps that's why his conscience began to trouble him.

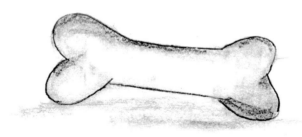

One day, he walked into the garden and approached the bush where I lay as usual, huddled in my nest of leaves and soil, and dangled a piece of rope in front of me.

"Come, Tilly," he said, and, because I wanted to please him, I crawled from my place under the bush and stretched my tired body as he attached the rope to my collar, the only thing left from my days of happiness with Sam. Even the collar was now dirty and ragged from the exposure to the cold and the wet in the garden. He led me out through the side gate, the first time I'd left the garden since arriving. Perhaps we were going for a walk.

I tried to wag my tail to show my appreciation, but it was so stiff from the months of coldness and lack of food that it barely moved.

I realized I wasn't going for a walk when the man picked me up in his arms and placed me in the back of his car, the one he'd used to bring me to the garden. I was afraid and wondered what was happening to me as the car drove along the roads, and I was tossed around in the back with nothing to help me keep my balance. After what seemed a long time to  me, the car stopped, and the man opened the tailgate and pulled me out, leading me by the rope.

Together, we walked up a long path and through a gate. I could hear many dogs barking, and my fears grew. What was going to happen to me next? I shivered again, not with the cold for once, but this time with a fear of the unknown. A large, wooden gate opened in front of us, and he led me through it into a courtyard where a woman stood waiting. My life was about to change; though as yet I didn't know how or why.

Chapter 2

Sanctuary

Within minutes of arriving at this new, strange place, I walked slowly, my head hung down, and my tail between my legs as the woman began to lead me towards a series of cages at the end of the courtyard.  Although I'd lived in the garden for months and had received so little in the way of love or attention, the man had been my last link with old Sam, and, in a way, I was sad and afraid to be left alone with a stranger. Most people don't realize how intelligent a dog can be, and I'd learned enough human speech to understand some of the words the man said to the woman who now held my leash. The words "unwanted," "can't keep her," and "no room in the house" meant something to me. I stood there shaking, a poor, bedraggled little dog who now felt confused and bewildered as the woman led me toward a shiny, metal gate with bars that led ... to where?

The woman had a kind face, and she spoke softly to me, the first words of kindness and softness I'd heard in a long time.

"Don't you worry, Tilly," she cooed. "Everything's going to be all right now. No one's going to hurt you. You're safe, little dog."

Most of the words were completely unfamiliar to me, but the sound of the woman's voice was soothing, and I allowed myself to relax a little as I realized that perhaps the woman could be trusted a little more than Sam's son's wife.

I still didn't wag my tail, that would be too much to ask, but I did at least prick up my ears as I saw what awaited inside the gate. There, ready and waiting just for me, was a lovely, warm, cozy bed. It was made of red plastic, not too posh, but it had a blanket inside it. In fact, when I drew closer, I saw not just one, but two blankets. Beside the bed sat a bowl full of fresh water for me to drink, and, perhaps most importantly of all, a bowl of food, real food, dog food, the sort that old Sam had

given me long ago, even though just a few short months previously.

In addition to the bed, the bowl of food, and the water, I noticed two toys lay on the floor of the pen. Toys! I hadn't seen a dog toy since I'd been taken from old Sam's house. One was in the shape of a bone; the other was a soft teddy bear, a little the worse for wear by the look of it, but a teddy bear, nonetheless. Things were looking up if this was to be my new home, which I thought it must be. But, would it last?

"There you are, Tilly. You make yourself at home," said the woman as she detached the rope lead from my tattered collar.

She said nothing more as she withdrew from the pen and left me to settle into my new surroundings. I sniffed at the food. It seemed okay. Another sniff, this time at the water bowl. That too appeared fine and would be my first drink of fresh water for some time.

However, I wouldn't touch anything at first. I suppose I was suspicious of such kindness, after the cruelty I'd experienced in recent months. I stood looking around at my new "home." All around me were similar pens to mine, each one with at least one or two dogs.

Barking continued around me, but, as the woman disappeared from view through a door into the building that stood on the opposite side of the courtyard, the racket slowly receded until a sort of quiet fell.

I walked to the bars that stood between the courtyard and me. I placed my nose through the gap that was just large enough for me to do so, and I sniffed the air. It appeared to hold no sense of threat, though there was a lot of tension present.

Dogs are very good at sensing things just by sniffing the air, and I, being an intelligent little dog (so others have said), was better than most. I knew that the tension came from dogs like me, brought to this strange place and left alone.

People other than the woman seemed to have things to do which involved entering and leaving the dog pens. Some held long-handled brooms, and some had buckets or large black sacks, but they all seemed to be friendly, and each spoke in calm and soft tones whenever they approached one of us dogs.

Perhaps because I just arrived, none of the people disturbed me on the first day, though a few stopped by to say hello through the bars of my pen. I realized that no one in this strange, new place was going to hurt me. Eventually I sniffed again at the bowl of food, took a mouthful, and enjoyed it so much that within minutes I'd greedily cleaned the bowl and washed the food down with a drink of water.

Feeling pleasantly full and exhausted, I tried out the inviting blankets in the bed. I pawed at them and arranged them into a nice comfortable heap, a shape that reminded me of the bed of leaves under the bush in the garden. I leaned over the side of the bed and took the teddy bear in my teeth, pulling it into the bed with me. I tucked the teddy under my chin, the way I used to do with the teddy bear that old Sam gave me. Within seconds of laying my tired and aching little body on the softness of the warm blankets and closing my eyes, I was fast asleep.

. . .

I didn't know it at that time, but old Sam's son had taken me to a local dog sanctuary, and I'd never have to go back to that cold and lonely life under the bush.

Around me were other dogs, many like me: unloved and unwanted. Some, many younger than I am, were in poor states of health. Older dogs had been cast out of their homes. Their owners didn't want an old dog around who might cost them money if it got ill.

The dogs soon told me why I was at the sanctuary, and I allowed myself to dream of the day when someone would come and find me and give me the love I craved. I promised myself that, if I was fortunate enough to find that person, I would love him with all my heart and be the best and most loving dog in the world.

For the present though, I slept the best and most comfortable sleep I'd enjoyed for months. No freezing-cold, dripping water landed on me from the branches of the bush, and no annoying insects crawled over me and made me jump up and scratch to get rid of them. No frozen earth dug into my ribs, and no woman of the house shouted at me for being there.

Chapter 3
New Beginnings

After a couple of weeks, I began to trust humans a little more. Each day, one of the women and sometimes the young boy who worked at the sanctuary took me out of my pen and put me on a lead. They took me through a side gate and into a wooded area that bordered the side of the compound. There, I could walk on grass, gravel, soil, and all the natural surfaces where dogs love to place their paws.

On the third day, the woman took me to the vet. I had an operation that one of the other dogs told me would prevent me from having unwanted puppies in the future. I felt a bit sore for a day or two but nothing too bad. I was given tablets for "worming" someone said, whatever that meant. They put  some drops on my neck that helped get rid of the nasty, itchy, little fleas that had bit me for ages.

A few days of good feeding, a warm bed, and regular walks made me feel so much better. I carried my tail higher as I walked, though my coat was still quite a mess. Although the lady who ran the sanctuary had tried

to comb and brush me, I was so afraid that any attempt to groom my coat hurt me and caused me to panic. I hated anyone touching me around my tail or back legs. The lady at the sanctuary decided that for now my coat could wait.

Lots of people arrived at the sanctuary daily, and I realized that they were looking at us, the dogs. Sometimes, one of the dogs would be taken from its pen, placed on a leash, and handed to one of these visitors, who led the dog away. Each time the people who worked in the sanctuary appeared pleased. It didn't take me long to understand that going with visitors must be a good thing.

Those dogs, of course, were going to new homes with people who would love and care for them. I didn't know it then, but my turn to be rescued was just around the corner.

After three weeks in the sanctuary, I began to put on a little weight, though I was still painfully thin. I desperately needed a home and someone to love me. I needed to run, to play, and to have a share of the freedom that many dogs experience every day.

One day an old lady came to the sanctuary and

seemed interested in adopting me, or so she said. She promised to come back after the weekend, but I never saw her again. I began to grow sad, thinking that no one wanted me, perhaps because of my scruffy, straggly coat and my thin, half-wasted body.

So many of the dogs at the sanctuary left with new owners, and I began to think that no one would ever want me and that I'd have to live in my pen for the rest of my life. I knew that the people at the sanctuary cared for me, as they did for all the dogs, but it wasn't quite like having a warm, cozy home to call my own and a loving family around me.

Winter began to give way to spring. The daffodils and tulips in the garden at the sanctuary started to poke their heads above ground. Then one day, my luck changed. A couple with two children arrived at the sanctuary and looked at all the dogs. When they came to my pen, I looked at them through my very expressive eyes, and tried my very best to wag my tail in a plea for them to notice me. They did.

"What a beautiful little dog," said the woman, and the two children agreed.

"She's a real scruff bag," said the man, but he said it with a smile on his face, as though my appearance didn't matter to him that much.

The man and the woman had kind voices, and they asked the woman from the sanctuary if they could take me for a walk in the woods. Soon, I found myself walking through the trees, my head moving from side to side, looking upwards as I tried to get a good look at the people who just might give me the home I needed so desperately.

I was happier than I'd been for weeks. They made such a fuss over me and really seemed to like me. When they held their hands in front of me, I eagerly licked them in a show of doggy friendship. I tried everything I could to make them want me.

I was sad when they returned me to the sanctuary and handed me back to the woman in charge. What I didn't know was that they would return the next day with their two dachshunds, to see if the little sausage dogs would accept me into their home to live with them. Over the next two weeks they visited me daily with their dogs, and I gradually got to know Sophie, the long-haired dachshund, and Candy, the smooth-haired one.

One day I was taken to the local dog groomer who sheared my matted fur. I ended up almost bald, even my head. It was the only way to get rid of the matted, tangled mess that my coat had become. Although it was for my own good, I admit I struggled through the entire session, and I'm sure the groomer was getting fed up with me. I shivered again when the groomer was finished. Though spring was here, I felt cold without my thick coat of fur. However, I did feel much better without the lank, hanging tresses that had trailed almost to the ground.

Back at the sanctuary the woman in charge saw

me shivering and placed a red, yellow, white, and blue doggie sweater on me to help keep me warm. I must have look very funny to everyone. The other dogs certainly thought so. I didn't care. At least it helped me to stay warm.

The reason for the grooming session became clear to me the next day when the couple arrived at the sanctuary once more, this time without Sophie and Candy. Instead, they had a beautiful, new red collar and matching leash with them and a bone-shaped metal tag with *MY* name and a new address engraved upon it. I was going to a new home at last.

They filled in some papers at the office and then walked me to their car. They gently placed me in the back, and I hate travelling in cars (they make me feel sick). This time, the ride was worth it because we arrived at what was to be my new home.

I felt strange at first, but I soon became accustomed to my new surroundings. Sophie, the long-haired dachshund, welcomed me with a wag of the tail.

Candy, the younger of the two (though she was eleven years old, Sophie being nearly thirteen), chased me through the house as if to say, "This is my home. You have to behave according to *my* rules if you're going to live here."

I didn't mind her chasing me. I could run faster than she, and it was good exercise for us both. I learned that Harry had rescued both Sophie and Candy, too, and they had been together all their lives. They came as a pair.

I settled in quickly, especially when I saw the soft, warm bed that my new owners had bought for me. It was a dark cherry-red, with a thick, padded mattress, and a warm blanket had been placed on top of the mattress as an added luxury. A cuddly, little teddy bear, something like the one I had when I lived with old Sam, sat in the bed. My tail wagged so fast with happiness it must have looked like the propeller of an airplane.

That night, I slept better than I had for a very long time. I'd been taken for a long walk, been well fed, played with a ball and a bone-shaped toy with Sophie and Candy in the garden, and been given many cuddles and pats by the couple and their children. When bedtime came, it took less than a minute for me to fall into a deep, deep sleep.

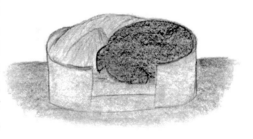

Speaking of bedtime, I was pleased that, like at old Sam's, my new owners took my bed upstairs, and I slept in their bedroom, with Candy and Sophie close by. The two dachshunds slept together in one large dog bed, but I had my own little spot in a corner of the bedroom.

Over the next few weeks, I learned to love my new family. They took me for lots of walks, and I was let off the lead to run and play in the fields near my new home. I loved chasing a tennis ball. I'd catch it, run around the field at top speed in a big wide circle, and then run back to the family members and drop the ball at their feet. That's still my favorite game. I never ran too far from my new owners, and always went back to them when they called my name. I wasn't going to risk losing my new family.

The only cloud that marred my first few weeks in my new home came one morning when Candy became very ill. I saw my new master take the little dog out to the car wrapped in a blanket. He had tears in his eyes. I knew that when humans had tears on their face it was a sign of great sadness. I heard the car drive away and a while later the man returned. Candy wasn't with him, and he cried even more. Something told me that like old Sam, Candy wasn't coming back. I wagged my tail and licked the man's hand to try and cheer him up. He stroked Sophie and me and made calm soothing noises, but it was clear to me he was very sad indeed.

For days, the man, the woman, the children, and Sophie showed their sorrow. I did my best to cheer them up, and, though it was clear that they all missed little Candy a lot, they knew that their new little dog needed them, too, as did Sophie.

Soon life retuned to normal, and Sophie and I became closer friends, as I tried to make up to the elder dachshund for the loss of her lifetime friend. Then, one Saturday, about two months after I'd arrived, a day out with the family brought about another great change in my life. I would meet Dylan.

Chapter 4

Completing the Pack

One very hot, sunny day in May, the family loaded me into the car once again and set off for an unknown destination. I hated the journey and was relieved when the car stopped and I was allowed to jump down from the  tailgate on to the firm ground. I shook myself, looked around, and felt a rising panic as I saw that I was back at the sanctuary. Was my family about to abandon me as I'd been abandoned once before? Had I done something terribly wrong without realizing it? I couldn't believe it and almost had to be dragged along on my leash as they all made their way to the familiar courtyard. My master, who I now thought of as 'Dad,' tried to reassure me, stroking and petting me, but I was still quite afraid as we all arrived at the door to the sanctuary office.

I needn't have worried, of course. They'd taken me back to have a small microchip injected below my skin to make sure that, if I ever got lost, I could be scanned with a special machine that would identify me and allow me to be returned to my owners. They must really love me.

Dad stayed in the office with me while the chip was inserted. *Boy, did that hurt.* I yelped, and Dad spent a couple of minutes comforting me and calming me. I

23

only hurt for a minute, and then it was as if nothing had happened. Mum and the children had gone to look at the other dogs in the sanctuary, and, when Dad and I emerged from the office, they were all looking at a little ball of fur huddled in the corner of one of the pens. There, shaking and quivering with fear, was a dog about my size, exactly the same color as me who looked a little like a sheep. He was obviously terrified.

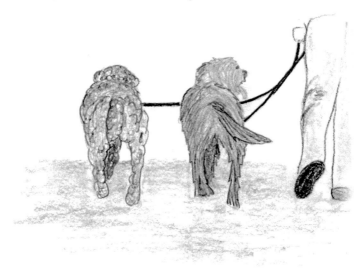

   Dylan, a Bedlington terrier (I'm half Bedlington), had been battered and abused. The family fell in love with him immediately. Dylan was taken from his pen and walked beside me in the familiar woods beside the sanctuary. I could sense his anxiety and fear and did my best to walk beside him and reassure him, wagging my tail and licking him as a sign of friendship. Though we had to leave him that day, I had a feeling it wouldn't be the last time I'd see Dylan. I was right.

Two days later, Dylan joined the family, and I had a new playmate. The two of us soon became great friends. We ran and chased each other on the field, while Sophie, who was getting a bit stiff with age, watched over us like a mother would. As you know, my favorite game, then and now, was to pick up a tennis ball in my mouth and be chased at full speed around the field, my tail swishing behind me as I ran. Dylan, who can run at the same incredibly fast speed as I, would join in happily, running and barking and jumping for joy.

The rest of that first year seemed to fly by, and Sophie, Dylan and I settled down to a happy life together with the family.

Just after Christmas, tragedy struck the home once more when poor Sophie became sick, just as Candy had a few months before. Again, Dad carried his beautiful dog to the car and left on a journey from which Sophie didn't return. As he arrived home once more with tears in his eyes, Dylan and I looked at each other and at him, and we wagged our tails at him in a sorrowful way as we licked his hands, and smelled Sophie's scent on him for what would be the last time.

With Sophie's death, Dylan and I lived together peacefully for a while, until the family decided to add to the dog pack once again. Over the space of a year and a half, Charlie, Penny, Alfie, and Molly all came to live in the family home, and I found myself taking over Sophie's job and playing 'Mother Hen' to the pack of terriers who now shared my home and my life.

Like me, all the dogs were all rescued, and each one of them has a story to tell of their incredible lives and their paths to becoming a rescue (rescued) dog. They have each added their stories to this series of books, but that, of course, as you humans say, is another story.

After a chance meeting between my Dad and something called a 'Canine Behaviourist', I began going to dog training classes with Dad. I learned to play fly ball, take part in agility work, which I absolutely adore, (I now hold the course record for doing it faster than anyone else), and to learn the basics of search and rescue work.

They've even taught me to find something called

'human DNA' whatever that is, simply by scent. I love doing the search work, and maybe one day I'll be able to find a real missing person or child and show everyone how useful a little rescue dog can be. Not bad for a little dog that no one wanted so short a time ago, eh?

The trainers tell all the newcomers to the classes that I'm the 'star pupil' of the class, and Dad and I are often asked to demonstrate various techniques and exercises for the benefit of those newcomers. The trainers sometimes have a laugh with my Dad and say that I'm the world's smallest Irish Wolfhound, because apparently I look a bit like one of those giants. In return, because I'm so small, Dad laughingly says I must be an 'Irish Wolf-Terrier,' and everyone has a fine giggle, and I join in by wagging my tail furiously.

I know that Dad's proud of me, whatever my ancestry, and I always try to do my best to please everyone as I race around the agility ring or go in search of whatever

I've been sent to find. When I'm not impressing people with my athletic abilities (I don't mean to brag), I spend my days sitting or lying beside Dad as he writes his books.

Mum bathes, grooms, and clips my coat regularly, keeping me looking smart and sleek. I trust her so much that I even let her clip and groom around my back legs and my tail, which are still sensitive and probably always will be. I know that Mum won't hurt me, and everyone says how pretty I look after a session on Mum's grooming table. After all, we girls do like to look our best, don't we?

I still play with my favorite tennis ball and run around the field in the company of any number of my new friends. Penny is especially good at playing games, and I'm trying to teach Alfie and Molly, the two newest members of the pack, to join in and play the way the rest of us like to play.

Charlie sometimes joins in, but he's greedy. When he gets hold of the ball, he runs around with it but won't give it back to Dad, or to anyone, and we all get bored standing around waiting for him to drop it. Silly dog!

By listening closely when they speak and observing their actions, I've taught myself to understand almost every word my family says. They all say that I'm a most intelligent little dog. I was eighteen months old when I was first adopted, and I'm now a happy, fit, and healthy four-year old.

Hey, I even won two rosettes at a fun dog show, for 'Best Rescue Dog' and 'Prettiest Bitch.' Wow, was I a proud little dog that day as I walked around the show ground with my two rosettes attached to my collar. Having found that which all rescue dogs seek most dearly, a loving and secure home, I know that I'll never again be a scruffy,  bedraggled, and unwanted dog. I have to boast that I'm the happiest little terrier in the world.

For me, the garden of my home is a place to play, to lie and relax in the sun on a beanbag, or just to sit beside Mum or Dad as they take a hard-earned rest. The garden of my nightmares, the bush under which I once slept and the hard, freezing ground on which I once laid my head, are now nothing but dim memories for me, and those memories recede further every day. I know that no one will ever kick me again or starve me or leave me out in the cold. Those days are gone, and only happy times lie ahead for me and the other dogs living with Harry and his wife.

I know how much they love me because earlier this year I had very sore paws and legs, and my fur had begun to drop out. Dad took me to the vet (he calls it the Doggie Doctor, and I humor him, because I do know what a vet is), and I had to take tablets for weeks. Not only that, but Dad had to put me in a little tub and bathe all four of my legs twice a day every day for weeks, and he never complained about having to do it. In return, I stood still in the water and let him lift my sore legs up one at a time to apply the special shampoo and rinse it off again afterward. Now that's love.

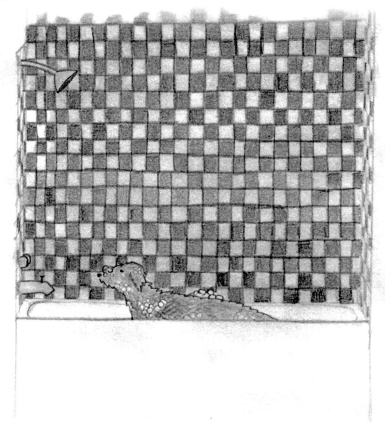

I love my family, and, though I hate to be left at home when they go out and bark to try to make them stay with me, it's only because I love them so much. I'm always a little afraid that, if they go, they won't come back one day, and I'll end up in the sanctuary as I did once before. The vet calls it 'separation anxiety' and says that I might grow out of it one day. The way I'm loved and cared for now would make any dog envious, and my heart leaps with happiness every day when I wake to see my family, human and canine, around me.

I can't possibly leave you without telling you my really big news. I'm a Mummy! Well, sort of. Just a few weeks ago my Mum and Dad went out and when they returned, guess what? They'd got a little tiny puppy with them. His name is Snoopy and he was just eleven weeks old. He is almost all white, but has a black and tan patch over one eye, which makes him look *so* cute. As you can imagine, he was very scared and a bit nervous when he first came into the house, what with meeting me and the others for the first time.

Anyway, I thought he needed looking after and so I decided to take him under my wing. I did something I don't usually do, well, actually *never* do. I let him sleep with me in *my* bed, and each night I make sure he's snuggled up tight beside me so that he'll feel safe through the hours of darkness. I play with him every day and try to teach him all the games I know. He's not as fast as I am of course, so when I run around the field for him to play 'chase,' I go a lot slower than usual. I run in much smaller circles than usual so that he doesn't get too tired. I have to look behind me from time to time to make sure he's there, and he always does his best to keep up.

I think he really does see me as his Mum now, and I do like looking after him. I suppose in a way it all goes with being 'Pack Leader,' but I do so love the little rascal.

The other day, a cocker spaniel we met on the field and tried to get a bit too boisterous with Snoopy, and knocked him over. Boy, did I give that spaniel a telling off? He won't do that to Snoopy again, I'm sure. I suppose as he grows up, Snoopy won't need me in quite the way he does now.

I'll always be around to protect Snoopy and all the members of the pack, which is just as well, because just a couple of days ago, Chloe the Cavalier King Charles Spaniel arrived, followed very quickly by Cassie, another little crossbreed terrier. Maybe you'll hear more of them later. I don't know much about her yet, but she sure is a very pretty little dog. So that's another one to add to 'my' pack and to be looked after when we're out, but never fear, Tilly's here, and as long I'm the leader of the pack, no one picks on Harry's dogs.

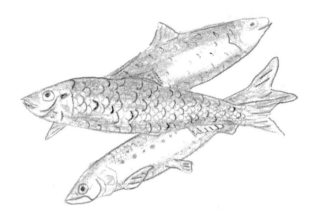

Oh, yes, before I go, let me tell you about our weekly treat, twice weekly actually. Along with our usual food, every few days Mum gives all of us dogs pilchards for tea. In case you haven't head of them, pilchards are little fish that live in the sea and taste just great. They are so tasty and yummy. So that's my life, at least so far, and I hope it might tell people how things can often look very bleak on the outside, but that good times may lie just around the corner. For me and the pack here at Harry's house that is certainly true.

Maybe my story will also encourage some people to understand that there are people out there who are not always as nice to us dogs. I know now that there are dog sanctuaries all over the world and that they all need help in their work to save dogs like me and Dylan and all the others. Our lives have been saved, and our futures are brighter thanks to Harry's family and those who work hard to find loving homes for dogs like us. We're not no-hopers, just no-homers in need of love and affection. Give us that, and we'll reward people with a lifetime of love in return.

This was my tale, and maybe one day I'll have more to tell, but for now I will ask everyone to excuse my happiness as I go on with the wonderful business of enjoying my life as 'Leader of the Pack' in the home of Harry the author and his wife and children.

My name is Tilly. Please don't forget me. I'm a rescue dog and proud of it.

Postscript

By Harry

There is no real ending to this tale, because, happily, Tilly's tale goes on from day to day. She continues to live contentedly with the author and his family and all the other dogs that make up the 'pack'. Every dog in the pack is a rescue dog, and each has his or her own remarkable tale of survival to tell. How they all ended up living with the author and his family can be found in the series of books that accompany this one. Harry Porter's Dog Tales relate the stories of Dylan, Charlie, Penny, Alfie, Molly, and Snoopy, the puppy, Chloe and Cassie, who joined us recently.

In the meantime, the author thanks you for reading this story but must leave you now, as Tilly has a tennis ball in her mouth, and it really is time to play…

About the Author

     Harry Porter's current series of books, Harry Porter's Dog Tales, are based on the real life stories of the six dogs that share the home of the author and his family. Every one of Harry's dogs is a rescue dog, that is, each has been subjected to a life of abuse, neglect or abandonment in one form or another before arriving at Harry's home.

     It is hoped that these stories will entertain, educate, and raise awareness among younger (and not so young) readers of the need for us as human beings to care for those animal friends who depend upon us so much and who ask for so little in return. A dog needs love, a home, a warm bed to sleep in, and someone to enjoy life with. As Harry says, and proudly displays the words on the baseball cap he wears to walk the dogs, "A rescue dog is a friend for life!"

     Harry Porter is a member or supporter of the following animal welfare organisations: The Mayflower Animal Sanctuary (UK), The Royal Society for the Prevention of Cruelty to Animals (R.S.P.C.A.) (UK), The Dogs Trust (UK), The American Society for the Prevention of Cruelty to Animals (A.S.P.C.A.) (USA), The Romanian Society for Preventing Cruelty to Animals (R.S.P.C.A.) (Romania) Harry Porter is the pseudonym of a respected thriller author whose works have gained him recognition and awards around the world.

www.Harry-Porter.webs.com

About the Illustrator

Mandy is a self-taught artist. She is an imaginative illustrator and painter who is driven by an incredible passion for self-expression through art. Her works are often noted for their unique style, elegance, technique and, vibrant colors. As soon as she was able to hold a crayon she knew art would always be a part of her life. Throughout her childhood, Mandy developed an appreciation for her beautiful surroundings. Years of artistic expression made it clear that her life would be centered upon her passion for art. Mandy is a professional artist full-time and enjoys illustration childrens books. She lives in Utah with her husband Andrew and two boys Alex and Connor.

www.MandyHedrick.com

Coming soon in the series,

Harry Porter's Dog Tales

Dylan's Tale
Charlie's Tale
Penny's Tale
Alfie's Tale
Molly's Tale
Snoopy's Tale
Chloe's Tale

Other 4RV titles from Harry Porter

Alistair the Alligator
Wolf!

Dylan's Tale

Written by Harry Porter
Illustrated by Mandy Hedrick

Acknowledgements

The series of books, Harry Porter's Dog Tales, of which this tale forms a part, owes much to the help of others who along the way have helped not just with supporting me in the writing and preparation of the books themselves, but also in the day to day business of working and living with our wonderful 'pack' of rescue dogs.

So I would like to say a big thank you to Brian Gallagher and the Canine Behaviourists of 'Dog Whispers', without whose help Tilly especially and many of the others would not be the dogs they are today. Thanks also to those often nameless volunteers who work and process and help to re-home the innumerable dogs that pass through the gates of dog sanctuaries, here and in other countries, every day of the year.

In particular I must acknowledge the work and the dedication of Jennie Foxall-Lord and those who work with her at The Mayflower Animal Sanctuary who care so deeply for all the animals in their care, and who helped place Tilly, Dylan and Charlie in our home.

I owe a debt of gratitude to Rebecca and Victoria, the first children to read and pass comment on the manuscripts. If they hadn't enjoyed them, these stories would never have reached a publisher.

To Vivian at 4RV, thank you for believing in Tilly and her gang, and to my agent Aidana, thanks for everything.

9 780981 868592